MW00944366

Gabriel Fernandez

A standalone story
of one of the 3,500 children
who are murdered by
their caregivers every year

Jessica Jackson

*For the purposes of anonymity, names of
siblings and friends have been changed
unless where commonly known*

**This book has details of child abuse
that some readers may find upsetting**

Every week in the UK
1-2 children are abused to death
by their parents or caregivers
In the USA, the number
is a staggering 27 children per week

*This is the story
of one of those children*

This work is based on a real case
*The first part of the story is semi-fictionalised,
with some events and dialogue added*

*The second part tells the facts of the case,
detailing the injuries, trials and sentencing*

Contents

Thank You For Choosing This Book

Hi, I'm Jess, and if you can spare a moment, I'd like to tell you a little about myself.

Working as a mental health advocate, and as a tutor and support worker for disadvantaged women, I've met with many of life's ups and downs. I've also lived through depression, eating disorders, abuse, and had my share of loss and grief.

Just as you may have.

But I was in shock when my friend confided in me that her grandson had been murdered by his mother, and I learnt that thousands of children are dying every year at the hands of their parents. I couldn't sleep for imagining their pain and terror. And so, it became my passion to raise awareness and work towards prevention, by writing the children's stories.

Please accept my apologies for the level of picture quality on enlarged photographs, the originals of which were taken by Gabriel's loved ones.

MY NAME IS GABRIEL FERNANDEZ

You're Writing What!?!

Many people ask me this question, and I know my books aren't for everyone, as they can be upsetting to read. Most of my friends can't read them – so thank you for picking up this book. I hope you'll 'enjoy' it.

Reader reviews get my books noticed – perhaps that's what brought you here – so I'd be very grateful if you could spare a moment to rate or review this book when you've finished reading.

I also have a free ebook for you — you can check it out overleaf ...

MY NAME IS GABRIEL FERNANDEZ

Your Free E-Book

Exclusive only to my readers

The tragic case
of Isaiah Torres

*(with bonus content on the short life
of Baby Brianna Lopez)*

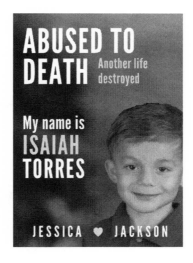

I'll let you know how to get your copy later

*(Royalties from my books go to
NSPCC, UNICEF and
Prevent Child Abuse America)*

MY NAME IS GABRIEL FERNANDEZ

My Name is Gabriel Fernandez

And this is my story …

(Dear Reader, please turn back a couple of pages for a short message from the author, and news of your FREE ebook)

'Gabe, come on, baby! Where are you?'

I clap my hand tightly over my mouth so they can't hear my giggles.

'I know where he'll be.' That's my big sister. She's five, and she knows everything.

I hear them whispering as three pairs of feet tiptoe towards my hiding place.

Poppa flings open the door. 'There you are!'

'Told you he'd be in the cubby,' says my sister.

Glad to be found at last, I burst out laughing.

But Poppa looks cross. 'We were starting to get worried about you.'

'I'm sorry, Poppa.'

Poppa smiles. 'It's okay, Gabrielito. As long as we know you're safe.'

My uncle Mike hugs me and grins. 'And we're ready to eat that cake!'

I've lived with my great-uncle Mike and his partner David since I was born, but it's just like living with a real Mommy and Daddy. So, I call Uncle Mike (Grandma's brother) Nonnie, and David is Poppa. I do have a real Mommy and Daddy, and I love them both; I just don't live with them. I'm glad I live with Nonnie and Poppa, because they tell me every day how much they love me.

When we get down to the kitchen, my big brother, Grandma Sandra and Grandpa Robert are waiting for us.

'What's he been up to this time?' says Grandpa.

'Nothing. Just playing.'

'Playing at being a naughty boy!' laughs Grandpa.

'I bet he was hiding in the cupboard,' says my brother.

Grandma shakes her head, but she's smiling too. 'Let's carry on with the party,' she says, and my brother moves to one side to show the biggest cake I've ever seen.

'That's for me?' I look up at everyone hopefully.

Nonnie Mike nods. 'Well, you'll want to share it with us!'

I dip my finger into the green frosting that makes a pattern around the edge of the cake. 'Mmm.' Even though it's February, it's warm enough here in LA to make the frosting drip down the sides.

'You can cut it now, Gaboo,' says Poppa David.

'And you can have the biggest piece,' says Grandpa. 'You're such a big boy now!'

'I can?'

Gabriel's uncles ensured his birthdays
were special

Grandpa nods, and Poppa grabs his camera. 'Hang on, I need a photo of this before the cake disappears!'

Nonnie leans across to help me cut the cake, and Poppa's camera clicks. 'This is a day to remember. Happy Birthday, Gabriel!'

We're all enjoying our cake and lemonade when Mommy comes through the door, with her boyfriend following behind. 'Hey, you started without me!'

'You're late,' says Grandpa.

'We waited for you, Mommy,' I say. 'But you didn't come.'

'What did you say to me?'

'Nothing, Mommy. Look, there's plenty of cake.'

She leans down and grabs my arm. Her nails dig in. 'I said I'd come, didn't I?'

'Yes, Mommy.'

She's still gripping my arm really tight.

'Leave him alone, Pearl,' says Nonnie.

'My boy, my rules.' But she lets go of my arm.

Poppa opens his mouth to speak, but then seems to think better of it. He squeezes my hand gently. It's best not to say anything when Mommy gets like this.

'Come on, Gaboo,' says Nonnie. 'Pass Mommy some lemonade.'

Mommy's boyfriend scowls. 'That stupid pet name you call him!'

'I like it,' I say softly.

'Look what you're doing to him!' says the boyfriend. 'Turning him into a faggot. The whole neighbourhood's talking about it.'

For the rest of the afternoon, I run around with my brother and sister, while the grown-ups talk. After a couple of hours, Mom licks the crumbs from around her mouth and leans down to kiss me. Her lips are sticky. 'Bye, son. See you soon. Come on, you two.' My sister and brother jump up and follow Mom out of the door.

Mom doesn't really walk; she struts like she wants everyone to watch her. And they do. When we're out in the street, or at the mall, people look at my mom, because she's beautiful.

§

A few days later, Nonnie and Poppa have another birthday treat for me – we're going to the fun-fair! My brother and sister are coming too, with Mommy and her boyfriend. The night before, I can hardly sleep for excitement. I love the merry-go-round and I know Nonnie will let me have lots of turns sitting up on the horses.

When Nonnie lifts me up for the third time, Mommy grabs his arm.

'You're spoiling him, Mike.'

Nonnie turns to her and raises his eyebrows.

'Come on, Gabe, get down,' says Mommy.

Nonnie starts to tremble. 'My baby can have as many turns as he wants.'

'*Your* baby!' says Mommy. 'There's just two things wrong with that. First, he's not your kid, and second, he's not a damn baby anymore!'

As Mommy puts me back on my feet, Poppa comes up to join us. 'What's going on?'

'You're making him soft. He shouldn't get his way all the time,' says Mom.

'It's for his birthday, Pearl! We want him to have fun, and remember this day when he's older.'

Mommy sighs. 'Anyway, two gay guys shouldn't be raising a kid. It's not right.'

'You're crazy,' says Poppa. 'We've given him a happy home, since you didn't want him!'

Mommy's boyfriend joins in. 'Look at him; he's already turning soft.'

Poppa shakes his head. 'Do you love your Nonnie and Poppa, Gaboo?'

I nod and grin. 'Of course I do. I love you both to the moon and back.'

'That's what I'm saying,' says Mom. 'He loves you.'

Nonnie and Poppa look confused. 'Of course he loves us. What do you mean?'

'You know what she means,' says Mom's boyfriend. 'You're turning him into a faggot!'

'I love you too, Mommy,' I say.

Christmas that year is the best one ever. I stay up late to watch the fireworks on Christmas Eve, and with everyone in our family gathered together, we eat every kind of tamales you can think of.

Excited to open his Christmas presents

Santa brings me a Ninja Turtles outfit and lots of other great presents, and at the end of Christmas Day, feeling so full we could burst, Nonnie, Poppa and me cuddle together on the couch and watch cartoons till we fall asleep. Just the three of us.

My name is Gabriel Fernandez and I am loved.

Grandpa and Grandma have come to visit, but they don't bring my brother and sister with them like they often do. I hear them tell Nonnie and Poppa they "want to talk".

'Go play in your room, Gaboo,' says Poppa, and I pick up my box of toy soldiers and scamper off.

Pretty soon their voices get louder.

'But he's our son, Robert. She didn't want him.'

'I know that, Mike. But she says two faggots shouldn't be raising that kid!'

'Don't call us that!' says Nonnie.

'I'm just telling you what she said.'

'Just because we love each other doesn't make us bad people. And no one loves Gabe more than we do.'

'I know that, Mike. We all love him,' says Grandpa. 'And we want the best for him.'

'You know how hard it is growing up gay, Mike,' says Grandma.

'But he's not gay!' says Nonnie. 'And he's only four years old!'

'I know,' says Grandma. 'I'm sorry, Mike. I didn't mean it. We don't know what to think.'

There's more stuff I can't hear until Poppa roars. 'That's a fucking lie! Who the hell's saying that? We're his parents; we love him like a Mom and Dad should. Nothing more!'

'It's just what we've heard, David.'

Nonnie starts to cry and I rush into the room.

'Don't cry, Nonnie.' I hug him and he holds me close.

'I'm sorry,' says Grandpa. 'But she's not going to stop this time. Sandra and I have been talking. We can take him.'

'No,' says Nonnie. 'No, he lives here with us.'

Grandma strokes Nonnie's arm. 'Listen, Mike. At least if he's with us, we'll all know he's being looked after. And you can see him as much as you want.'

'But he belongs here,' says Poppa quietly.

'You've given him a good home,' says Grandma. 'But maybe the time's right.'

Nonnie and Poppa look tired.

'Pack his things and we'll pick him up at the weekend,' says Grandpa.

I can feel Nonnie shaking, and he's making my t-shirt wet. 'It's okay, Nonnie,' I say. 'Don't cry.'

'We'll see you then,' says Grandpa.

Grandpa and Grandma come on Saturday, just like they said they would.

'It won't be for long,' says Poppa, as he prises my arms from around his neck. 'And we'll see you all the time.'

Nonnie stands back, crying like his heart is breaking.

I run to him for a hug. 'I'll see you tomorrow, Nonnie. Won't I?'

He nods. But he looks sick and older somehow. Not my laughing, lively Nonnie.

'Let him go, Mike,' says Grandpa, and he takes my hand and helps me get into the car.

Grandma tries to give me some candy, but I don't want it. I just want my Nonnie and Poppa.

'You can stop waving now, Gabe,' she says. 'They can't see you anymore.'

I wipe my eyes and keep waving.

§

Things are pretty good at Grandma and Grandpa's. I love them to bits, and they give good cuddles too. Especially Grandma. But I sometimes think about Nonnie and Poppa in their house, and me here in this house, and I wish we could still be together. When they come to visit, I want to go home with them, and I cry for a little while afterwards. But then I get busy with my chores and playing with my brother and sister and my cousins, and I feel okay again.

Gabriel adored the Teenage Ninja Turtles

There's even a pool at Grandma's house! When us kids all jump in, nearly all the water jumps out! I've learnt how to swim, and I love it when we're all together and Grandpa puts pork chops on the grill and lets me help him, and says I'm his clever boy. I love riding my bike too, and I've taught my cousin how to ride his. Now we can take off down the street, with Grandma calling after us to stay on the sidewalk and look out for people and cars.

We're a big, noisy, fun family, and I love everybody! I didn't tell you about my Daddy yet. He's big and strong and they tell me I look like him. I'm cool with that. When we see him, he gives us presents and lifts me up onto his shoulders and carries me around that way. Even though it's a bit scary, I like it because he's my dad. My uncles and aunties and cousins are real nice too. Some of my cousins are already grown up, and yes, I guess they spoil me.

We have great birthday parties and us kids can run about and do just about whatever we want. We get to stay up late, and if my brother and sister are spending the night, we talk and giggle in bed until Grandma comes to tell us to shush. Then I reach up my arms to her and she hugs me and whispers that I'm her Gabrielito.

Whenever Mommy comes to visit, I hear Grandpa whisper something to Grandma. It sounds like: 'Don't leave him alone with her,' and I think they mean me. It's weird, because even though she's my mommy and I love her so much, I don't really like being on my own with her, so I'm glad Grandpa says that.

Mommy doesn't give hugs like everyone else. She squeezes real hard and her long fingernails jab into my skin; on my arms or at the back of my neck. I try not to yell because she's my mommy and I know she doesn't mean to hurt me.

I live with Grandma and Grandpa for about three years. And I'm so lucky, because everybody loves me. I still see Nonnie and Poppa, and Mommy and her new boyfriend. Things are pretty great. But one day, Mommy and my grandparents are arguing real loud.

Mom's yelling. 'He's my kid. He's legally mine, Dad, and I want to raise him. I want to bond with him; I want the chance to have a relationship with my son before it's too late.'

'But you didn't want him, Pearl,' says Grandma. 'And he's settled here with us.'

'Well, I want him now!' says Mom. 'I'm his mother.'

Grandpa lowers his voice. 'You can see him whenever you want, Pearl. Come on; you get the best of everything this way.'

'No! I've decided.'

'Don't take him, Pearl. Please, don't take him.' I think Grandma is crying.

'He's coming to live with me and Tony, and you can't do nothing about it!'

'You just want that welfare check!' says Grandma. 'Don't think we don't know that!'

Mom hesitates for a moment. 'I want to bond with my son!' she yells. 'And I've got the legal right to take him!'

It seems like Mom is right. She's got the law on her side and I have to go live with her.

§

It's great to be with my brother and sister all the time, and we have a lot of fun playing in the apartment, until Tony or Mommy tells us to shut the fuck up.

I'm sad when I realise that Mom doesn't want to bond with me after all. I always seem to get on her bad side, even though I try my best to be good.

And when Tony hits me for the first time, I get dazed for a while. I've been smacked before, of course. You don't get to be seven without being naughty sometimes. But Tony's a big, powerful guy, and he doesn't hold back like you're supposed to with little kids. I look at Mom, but she just kinda nods and I know she won't be stopping him. Tony's real name is Isauro, by the way, but everyone calls him Tony.

You never really know where you are with him. Sometimes he's having fun with you, maybe teasing or something, and you'll be giggling and rough-housing and suddenly he'll go serious, and make out you've done something wrong, even though he started the game in the first place. It's got so I don't want to join in, but then he pesters me and pretends to slap me, and then the slaps get real, and they get harder and harder until they really hurt. If I cry, he calls me a cry-baby and says that I'm gay. So I don't really know what to do. I just want to stay out of his way.

I've been hit more times since I came to live with Mommy and Tony than the whole time I was with Nonnie and Poppa, or Grandma and Grandpa. And that belt really hurts too. They've told us not to tell about the beatings, or we'll get hurt even worse.

In February though, we have a big birthday party for me, and I love it because everyone comes; my cousins, my grandparents, and most special of all, Nonnie and Poppa. It's a great day, and it reminds me of when I was happy all the time. But when the party's over, I can't stop myself from crying, so I go and lie on my bed until I fall asleep. I wish I could live with Nonnie and Poppa, or Grandma and Grandpa again.

Nonnie looks so thin now. If I lived with him I could take care of him. I'm going to ask Mommy if I can do that.

Mommy punches me in the face when I ask her.

The next day, I have to go to school with a black eye. My teacher is Miss Garcia. She asks me what happened, and when I tell her I walked into the closet door, she doesn't smile and say how clumsy I am, she puts her hands on her hips and asks if I'm sure. I nod and continue helping her to pick up the crayons that have fallen on the floor.

'Gabriel, you can tell me anything, you know.'

'I know, Miss.'

§

A few days later, things have gotten a whole lot worse at home.

'Can I stay and help you tidy up again, Miss?'

'Of course you can, Gabriel,' says Miss Garcia. 'Why don't you go and collect all the writing books?'

'Okay.' But I don't want to leave her side.

'Gabriel?'

I look up at her.

'Do you want to tell me something?'

I nod. 'Is it normal for a mom to beat you with a belt?'

'Does your Mommy do that, Gabriel?'

I take a deep breath. 'Only sometimes. But it makes me bleed.'

She squats down in front of me and takes both my hands. 'No, it's not normal, honey.'

'Oh. I just wondered. You won't tell her I told you, will you?'

'I don't know, Gabriel. I'll have to tell someone.'

'But not Mommy, or Tony!'

'Come and sit beside me.'

She pulls two chairs together in the reading corner, and takes my hands again. 'I won't tell your mom or Tony, but this isn't right, Gabriel. You know that don't you, sweetheart?'

'I guess so.'

'And you want it to stop, right?'

'As long as Mommy doesn't get into trouble or hurt or anything.'

'I think someone will just talk to her, Gabriel. And they'll want to ask you some questions too. Just to get this all straightened out. So it doesn't keep happening.'

I think about it for a little while.

'How does that sound, Gabriel?'

'Okay, I guess. Can we sit here for a few more minutes, Miss?'

'Sure, Gabriel.' And she puts her arm round me and I can feel the softness of her sweater and smell its freshness.

'Sometimes I feel scared to go home, Miss Garcia.'

'You do, honey?'

I nod into her chest and start to cry.

'Oh, baby,' she says, and pulls me in closer. 'We'll get this all sorted out, don't you worry.'

That evening, a lady comes to visit. Mom lets her inside and they talk for a while. She comes again, a few times after that, and Mom tells us kids not to tell her anything if she asks. For a while, instead of punching me in the face, Mommy and Tony just hit my arms and legs. I know that if they think I'm naughty I have to be punished, but they seem to enjoy hurting me now. I don't understand that part of it. They use a bat sometimes and they knocked out two of my teeth. It hurt so much, and I got the belt for crying too loud.

I've started writing notes that I leave around the house for Mom to read because I guess she feels I don't love her enough.

When a volunteer lady stops by one day, Mom thrusts my notes at her as she's leaving. I wish she wouldn't do that because they're private. On one I wrote: 'I love you until you die.' And on another: 'I love you so much that I will kill myself.' If it would make Mom happy, I would do that. Because I seem to make her mad just by being around. No matter what I try, she stays mad a lot of the time.

The lady looks shocked when she reads what I've written, but Mom explains the notes by saying I want to go back to live at Grandma's, and I can't tell if the lady believes her or not, but she makes a phone call and passes the phone to Mom. They ask Mom some questions and Mom says I'm doing okay right now, and there's no risk of me killing myself. I'm not sure how they decide that without talking to me.

One morning soon after, a cop comes to our door. Mom and Tony try to hide me away at first because of the bruises, but when I get called out of the bedroom, the officer doesn't seem to notice them. He takes me down to his car and I decide I'm going to tell him everything. Even about the cigarettes they put out on my skin. Not everybody likes cops, but I know they're there to keep us safe, and he's going to help me for sure. But when he turns to face me he looks angry instead of kind.

'Right, Gabriel,' he says. 'You've got to stop all these silly games. You're worrying your parents to death. We know you're telling lies, and you're just trying to get back to stay with your grandma and grandpa. Well, you can't. You live with your mom and stepdad and that's where you'll stay. You got that?'

All I can do is nod.

'And if you carry on with these lies about them hurting you, I'll be taking you to jail. We know you're just acting up to get attention. You're just a spoiled kid who wants his own way all the time.'

I swallow hard.

'So, no more lying, or it's the jailhouse for you.'

'Yes, Sir.'

§

'Get this place cleaned up, Gabriel!'

It's always best to jump up as soon as Mom says that, so I go into the kitchen for the mop and bucket. The bucket's heavy when it's full and I slop a little onto the floor where I shouldn't.

Mom screams at me, and drags me by my ear into her room. 'I need to teach you a lesson.' And she reaches for the air-gun they keep near the bed.

I try to decide whether it's safer to try and run out of the room or do as she tells me, but as usual she's one step ahead of me.

'Don't you move, Gabriel.'

As Mom lines up the gun with my face, I screw up my eyes and clench my fists, and think of Nonnie and Poppa, and how they used to hug me and call me their sweet little Gaboo. But when the pellet hits, the pain is like nothing I've ever felt before.

'Don't cry,' she says.

I try to hold back the sobs that are rising in my throat.

'And don't tell nobody, right?'

I daren't open my mouth in case the scream comes out.

'Right, Gabriel?'

I nod.

'Get in that cupboard,' she says.

I look around. She's pointing to the cubby at the foot of the bed.

'But I can't ...'

She whacks me with the belt that hangs on the back of the door. 'Get in.'

I'm only small but I still have to struggle into the tiny space.

'Wait till Tony gets back and I tell him about the mess you made on my floor.' And I hear her heels click-clacking out of the bedroom.

My whole body is aching, and my face stings like crazy where the pellet from the air-gun hit. I know Mom told me not to cry, but I can't help it. I'm frightened and I don't know what's going to happen next.

When I can't stand it any longer, I manage to push one of the doors open a little bit, so that I can move my position slightly. A short while later, I hear my sister asking where I am, and Mom tells her I'm being punished, but she doesn't tell her I'm in the cupboard.

Mom must have taken off her shoes because I don't hear her creep into the room before she smashes the door against my toes. She doesn't say anything, but I hear her fix something onto the outside of cupboard door.

'Mom,' I whisper. 'Mom, can I come out now? I'll clean up and be good.'

She bashes the door. 'Shut the fuck up. I'm not finished with you yet.'

My name is Gabriel Fernandez and I'm scared.

I say my prayers but I don't know if God can hear me. *Nonnie, Poppa, Grandma, Grandpa, please come get me.*

I imagine their hugs and kisses. I know they still love me even though Mommy doesn't let them see me so much anymore. The last time I saw Nonnie, he told me how much they miss me, and he looked sad.

I put my arms around his neck and told him not to worry, because when I'm old enough I'll go back and live with them again. Nonnie smiled, but there were tears coming down his cheeks. He'd gotten really thin, and I told him I wished I could make him some soup, like he used to make for me when I got sick.

Unconditional love

Suddenly I hear Mom's voice again. 'Yeah, it was really funny.'

She seems to be in a good mood now.

'You can try it when you get home. When are you coming? I miss you, baby.'

Oh, she's on the phone.

'Right in the face! I know, and now he's in the cubby. He tried to get out but I locked him in.'

It goes quiet while Tony speaks.

Mom laughs. 'Sure, if you want to. He's my kid, we can do whatever we want.'

It's late when Tony gets home, but it seems he can't wait to come and see me. Maybe he's going to let me out.

The light from room dazzles me when they open the door of the cubby.

'I didn't think he'd fit in there,' laughs Tony.

She snorts. 'He doesn't!'

'Get him out then,' says Tony.

My skin scrapes along the edges of the cubby as she drags me out. I land on the floor.

'Up,' says Mom, and hoists me up by my arm.

My legs won't hold me.

'Stand up like your mother says or I'll beat the living crap out of you,' says Tony.

I reach for the edge of the bed, and he slaps my hand away.

'Cheat!' he says. 'Do it by yourself.'

When I'm finally on my feet, he takes my chin in his hand and squeezes. 'Fucking hell, Pearl, that's a pretty bad mark on his face. What's that nosy old teacher gonna say?'

'I was thinking we could shoot somewhere else,' says Mom, pointing to my pee-pee.

Tony roars with laughter. 'That's my girl. Still, better keep him off school a couple of days.'

'He's too dumb to learn much anyway,' says Mommy, as she punches my arm.

'Please don't hurt me anymore, Mommy.' My throat is so dry I can hardly speak. 'Please, Mommy.'

'Did you hear something just then, Tony?'

'Not a thing. This kid wouldn't dare tell you what to do, would he, honey?'

'He knows better than that! You want to have some fun with the gun now, Tony?'

'Hey, I'm tired right now. Let's get something to eat first.'

I cry as he stuffs me back inside the cubby and fits the piece of wood across the handles.

'Hey, Gabe.'

I must've have fallen asleep because I wake up and bang my head on the side of the box.

'I got you something.' My sister pushes a piece of banana through the tiny gap in the door.

There isn't enough room to move my arms so I can't get hold of it. It smells beautiful. 'A bit to the left,' I say, and manage to get my mouth around it. 'Anything to drink?'

'I'll try and get you some juice later.'

Soggy bits of banana are stuck around my lips and I can't lick them off. There'll be hell to pay if they find out my sister's been feeding me. 'Can you get your hand through to wipe my mouth?'

She pushes a finger in and I kind of move my face around.

'Thanks.'

'I'll see if I can get the juice now.'

But soon I hear Mom yelling at her, and my sister doesn't come back.

Nonnie, Poppa, can you hear me crying for you? Please come and get me. I just want to go home with you.

§

Mom has to sort out some money problems at the welfare office, so us kids troop along behind her. It's a hot day, and as usual the men on the street are staring at Mom and whistling, because she's almost showing her boobies and her skirt is very short.

For once I'm glad they shaved my hair off because even now the sweat is trickling down my neck.

We have to wait around for a little while, and I notice the security guard is watching me. I turn away, but when I turn back, he's still looking, but kind of smiling. I smile back. I think he's trying to tell me something, but he's too far away. Mom has a tight hold of my hand, but I slowly try to move us a bit nearer to the man, and I can see that he's mouthing the words: 'You okay?' And again: 'You okay, buddy?'

They're calling Mom's name to go into the interview room, so I quickly make my hand into a fist and kind of nod my head towards Mom. The man gives a thumbs up sign, and mouths: 'Don't worry,' as I'm dragged along into the room.

After that, the cops come by again, but nothing changes.

§

'Hey, Gabriel.'

'Auntie!' It's Mom's little sister.

'How's it going, Gabrielito? You look kinda tired.'

'Oh, I'm okay.'

'You sure about that, Gabe? Looks like you've been getting hit.'

When someone is kind to you, it makes you want to cry and I know my lip is trembling. 'Mom hit me. In my eye.'

My auntie sighs. 'Come here, Gabe.' She hugs me, and I don't flinch where she touches my bruises, because I like her holding me.

'I'm going to take your photo, sweetheart,' she says.

'But I've got this fat lip and I can't open my eyes properly.'

'You still look gorgeous. Come on.'

I used to love having my photo taken with Nonnie and Poppa. They've got heaps of photographs of me smiling into the camera.

'Gabe, I'm worried about you.'

'I'm alright, honestly.' I know Mom will kill me if she thinks I've been talking. 'Please don't say anything to Mom or Tony.'

'I won't. It doesn't do any good anyway. But I might tell someone else and show them your photo. How'd that be?'

I'm still scared, but I nod. 'But if I could just show Mommy how much I love her, I think everything would be alright.'

She shrugs. 'Maybe.'

We hear Mom moving around in the kitchen.

Auntie whispers into my ear. 'And I'm going to see if they'll let me sleep over so you won't get hurt so much.' She pushes me away so Mom won't see us cuddling each other.

When my auntie isn't here, they make me go inside the box most nights, and sometimes during the day too. I can hardly breathe because they stuff a sock in my mouth and wrap tape around it. I hate the handcuffs they put on my ankles; my skin is coming off where they scrape against it. I told Mom they were too tight, but she just laughed and hit me with the belt.

When I'm in here, I try to think of nice things. I think about all the old photos Nonnie and Poppa used to take, and I pretend I'm back with them.

There's one photo where I'm just a baby and I've got my toe right up in my mouth, and even though I'm crying with pain right now, I can still smile about that one!

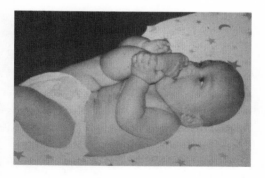

The cutest baby

And there's the ones where we're on the merry-go-round, and the ones at Christmas. We were so happy then. I wasn't scared. I was safe.

And then with Grandma and Grandpa; that was great too. Grandpa used to play the Big Bad Wolf and chase us around the room until we were giggling so much we all fell on the floor. But now I'm locked in a small cupboard and I can't call out for help from the social work lady who comes to check that I'm okay.

When they're putting their cigarettes out on me, Mom tells me that she didn't want me, and Tony calls me gay. That's when two men love each other, like Nonnie and Poppa. But Tony says it like it's a terrible thing. Maybe Mom and Tony didn't feel loved when they were little kids, and it makes them act all weird. I guess that's one for the shrinks. But I wish they'd look into it soon, because I keep getting hurt.

§

For Mother's Day, we make all kinds of cool stuff at school. I want to make sure my Mom knows just how much I love her, so when Miss Garcia hands out cards and we can put our own photo inside, I'm buzzing with excitement. On the front of the card there's a drawing of a house, and the words say: 'Open the door to see who loves you.' I think Mom will love me back a little when she sees it. I also write that she's a loving mom, and that I love her because she's beautiful. We have coupons too, and we can write all the things we want to do to help our Moms. I write, as neatly as I can: I will be good. I will clean the dishes. A time for me and you.

My name is Gabriel Fernandez and I love my mom.

I have to spend a long time in the cubby nowadays. I sometimes feel like I can't breathe, and I start thinking about dying again, to make Mommy happy.

My brother and sister aren't allowed to come and see me, but one day when Mom and Tony aren't home, my brother presses his face against the box. 'We love you, Gabrielito,' he says. And I start to cry and almost choke.

'It's going to be okay,' he says. 'If I can get to see Grandma I'll tell her how bad it's gotten. I …'

Someone is coming up the steps to the apartment, and my brother jumps up. 'I'm going to play something for you, Gabe,' he whispers before running from the room. 'It's just for you, bro.'

A few minutes later I hear my favourite song coming over the stereo.

'Turn that down!' yells Mom.

But I smile, because it's a message from my brother. Shine Bright Like A Diamond. I'll try. I'll try to keep going and I won't die. Because help is coming; I just know it.

§

'Mom,' I say one day when I'm out of the cubby and the house is quiet, and Mommy seems to be in a good mood. 'Why do you let Tony hurt you?'

'Don't be crazy, Gabriel. It's nothing. And I give as good as I get.'

'I know, but ...' She still seems to be calm so I decide to carry on. 'I want you to be safe, Mom.'

'Mmm.' She's not really listening.

'It might be better if it was just you and us, Mom.'

Now she's listening. 'So you're telling me to leave the man I love! Who do you think you are?'

'I didn't mean it like that, Mom.' But I guess I did.

Later, my sister and me are playing in her room. She's got a new doll to show me, and I try to be excited for her but I'm just so tired. I don't sleep too good anymore, especially if they've put me in the cubby.

Suddenly, Tony bursts through the door, and punches me right in the face. 'Don't tell your mom to leave me! Don't you dare! You got that?'

'I didn't mean to, Tony. It's just that you hit her sometimes, and it hurts her.' I know he will hurt me more, but I have to protect Mommy.

Tony's face seems to turn black. 'Don't tell me how to be around my girlfriend! You little faggot!' And he drags me away from my sister and into their room.

I hope I'm not going back into the cubby.

They don't put me back in there, but instead they beat me real hard for a very long time.

My name is Gabriel Fernandez.
And I was abused to death.

Everyone seems to know about me now. In the UK, it's Baby P, and in the US, it's me. But there are thousands of kids like us dying every year. The strange thing is, lots of grownups get all fired up about the death penalty for people like Mom and Tony, but they still think it's okay to whup their kids, and nothing really changes.

They made a documentary called The Trials of Gabriel Fernandez. It's a clever name, because it means the trials of abuse I was put through with Mommy and Tony, but it also shows their actual trials, in the court-room.

On the TV, Grandpa gets up on the witness stand in the court-room, and he sobs.

My uncle George and auntie Elizabeth say nice things about Nonnie and Poppa and I wish I could reach down and hug them for saying that.

They interview lots of people, including Poppa David. He was sent back to El Salvador, because he wasn't really allowed to be in the USA. I can see the grief in his face and hear it in his words.

With Poppa David – Grandma Sandra – Nonnie Mike

As for Nonnie Mike, I think he kind of gave up after I died. He got so thin and the joy went out of him. Pretty soon, he died of cancer. Grandma Sandra was the next to pass, when her diabetes had made her real sick. And when coronavirus hit the world in 2020, Poppa caught it and died. So none of us lived very long, but at least we are together again.

My name is Gabriel Fernandez.

Thank you for reading my story.

It's time to hand over to Jessica again, who now tells a more factual **account of my life and death** …

Why Did They Murder Gabriel?

Gabriel Fernandez
20.02.05 - 24.05.13
aged 8 years & 3 months
Los Angeles, California

Gabriel's mother, Pearl Fernandez, had four children with Arnold Contreras.

After their third child was born in February 2004, Pearl complained that he had caused her too much pain during delivery, and refused to care for him, leaving him with Arnold's parents in Texas. Fortunately for that little boy, his paternal grandparents adopted him, and Pearl, Arnold and their two older children moved back to California, where Gabriel was born.

Around four years after Gabriel's birth, Pearl's fifth child, a daughter, was born to a different man. The little girl's father found his girlfriend to be a neglectful mother, and when she threatened to cut the baby's throat as she wouldn't stop crying, he decided he'd had enough and left, taking the baby to live with him.

From the beginning, Fernandez was a reckless and uncaring mother. When just a baby, her first born son was injured in a car accident as he wasn't wearing a seat belt. A relative reported her, saying that she also beat the three-year-old, but the investigation soon stalled.

And once again, with Gabriel, Pearl did not want her newborn, but his great-uncle Michael and his partner David collected Gabriel from the hospital, and gave him a loving family home for the first three-four years of his life.

These early years were filled with happiness; you only need to look at the many photos on the internet to see the love and contentment he shared with Michael and David. Heartbreakingly for the little family, they faced escalating prejudice over Gabriel being raised by a gay couple, and feeling that they had no choice, Michael and David reluctantly allowed the little boy they called their son to go and live with his maternal grandparents.

With those who made him feel safe and happy

For a further three years, Robert and Sandra Fernandez gave Gabriel a stable home. But when their grandson was six, Pearl claimed that she wanted the opportunity to bond with her son, and that she had a legal document giving her custody. And so Gabriel was removed once again, to live with his mother, and her boyfriend, Isauro Aguirre (known as Tony), along with Gabriel's older brother and sister.

Although their caregivers were harsh and neglectful to all three children, they were soon singling out the gentle and sweet-natured Gabriel as the target for the most intense torture.

Gabriel's brother and sister described how he was tied, gagged, beaten with a belt, shot in the face and groin with a BB gun (a type of air-gun that shoots lead or metal balls) and had his teeth knocked out with a bat.

Although he had a bed in his brother's room, Gabriel was often locked in a small cabinet, nicknamed 'the box', in his mother and her boyfriend's room, with his ankles handcuffed together, a sock shoved into his mouth and a bandana tied over his face. He would frequently spend several hours a day in the cubby, as well as most of his nights. Gabriel had to eat cat litter, and had cigarettes burned onto his skin. He was forced to have cold baths, while simultaneously being pepper sprayed, and was made to wear girls' dresses, while his mother and her boyfriend yelled at him that he was gay.

On the day of the fatal beating, Gabriel and his sister were playing in her room with her toys, perhaps including her dolls, which would have given Fernandez and Aguirre ammunition to once again accuse the little boy of being gay. After they started hitting him, they dragged him into their room and locked the door.

§

Late in the evening of 22 May 2013, dispatchers received a call from a woman in Palmdale, Los Angeles, saying: "My son is not breathing". That woman was Pearl Fernandez.

The fire and ambulance personnel who were first on the scene were shocked at what they saw. At first, they thought the little boy was suffering from a rare disease, as Gabriel had such an array of injuries, including swollen ankles, strangulation marks around his neck, abrasions to his skin, burned left palm, bite marks, and bruising from head to toe. Gabriel was in cardiac arrest, so they performed CPR and managed to stabilise him.

Emergency crews said that neither Gabriel's mother nor stepfather seemed to be upset, nor did they ask if they could accompany their son to the hospital, with Pearl appearing to be more concerned about the welfare of her cats. Gabriel's siblings had been told to support the story their caregivers gave to the paramedics; that they'd been playing, running round the coffee table, and their brother had fallen and hit his head. (Pearl also gave another version of her story, that Gabriel had slipped in the bathtub, adding that some of the injuries were caused by self mutilation.)

On arrival at Antelope Valley Hospital, staff were able to get a pulse, and when it faded again, Gabriel was resuscitated. Medical practitioners added to the list of injuries already noted by the emergency personnel: depressed skull fractures, which were crunchy, like Rice Krispies, black eyes, missing skin on his neck, apparent burns on his throat, cuts above his penis and reddened base of penis, ligature marks on his ankles, bullets (from the BB gun) in his lung and groin, cigarette burns, and various cuts and abrasions all over his body, in various stages of healing.

Gabriel was put on life support, then transferred to the children's hospital.

§

The following day, Detective Elliott Uribe (from Los Angeles County Sheriff's Department) interviewed Isauro Aguirre, asking, "What happened that night in the bedroom?"

And as countless child murderers before and since, Aguirre replied: "**I spanked him**".

Uribe went on to ask him: "Why?"

Aguirre replied that Gabriel had said to Pearl that Aguirre was always hurting her, and that if she left him, he would start being good. But then, when questioned by Aguirre, Gabriel told him that he hadn't said that at all. And that made Aguirre angry. He admitted punching Gabriel 20 times in the body and 10 times in the face.

Uribe asked about the level of anger he was feeling that night, on a scale of one to ten. Aguirre replied that it was at level 20, and that he saw red.

When Gabriel's life support was turned off the following day, 24 May 2013, Fernandez and Aguirre were charged with intentional murder in the first degree, involving the infliction of torture; the latter 'special circumstance' allowing for the consideration of the death penalty. Aguirre was keen to fight his case, as he felt that his hands were clean. He said: "They want me to sign a paper for something I haven't done. I know in my heart, mind and soul that I am innocent".

The autopsy report gave the cause of death as blunt force trauma, along with neglect and malnutrition.

§

The case might have been lost amongst the many child murders by parental abuse that occur in the US, but journalist Garrett Therolf of the LA Times heard about the case and began to follow it up, asking himself: "How had a child who was known to DCFS (Department of Children and Family Services) come to be so severely abused?"

Therolf found that it was hard to get to the truth in the sprawling organisation that seemed to be bound not merely by privacy, but by secrecy. But he managed to track down an employee who had access to a confidential internal report into child abuse, and was willing to allow Therolf access to information, in an effort to discover the truth about Gabriel's case.

Unsurprisingly, a list of injuries and threats to Gabriel and his siblings was found, and Therolf decided to make sure that Gabriel's story was told.

§

Due to Pearl Fernandez' perceived intellectual disability, she could not face the death penalty, whereas Aguirre had no such protection. Therefore, the pair could not be tried together, as had initially been planned.

Four social workers involved with the family were also due to be tried, with the charges against them including child abuse and falsifying public records.

LA County DA, Jackie Lacey, felt they had a case to answer, because they did intentional things that kept Gabriel in harm's way: "We believe these social workers were criminally negligent and performed their legal duties with wilful disregard for Gabriel's well-being ... They should be held responsible for their actions".

§

More than four years after Gabriel's death, the trial of Isauro Aguirre began on 16 October 2017, under presiding judge, George G Lomeli.

Aguirre's defence attorneys contended that their client was under the influence of Fernandez, and had acted in a moment of blind rage; that he exploded and didn't intend for Gabriel to die.

Deputy DA for LA County, Jonathan Hatami, led the prosecution team, whose job was to prove that Gabriel's murder was an intentional act. Hatami (himself a survivor of child abuse) gave a poignant opening statement, pointing out that Isauro Aguirre was a 32 year old man, 6' 2" tall, weighing 270 lbs.

In contrast, eight year old Gabriel was 4' 1" and 59 lbs.

§

The medical experts who were called to the witness stand gave damning testimony.

Coroner Dr James Ribe took two days to document all of Gabriel's injuries. He had observed shrinkage to the little boy's thymus gland to less than half its expected size, showing that Gabriel had been under severe emotional and physiological stress for several months.

Reporting that Gabriel's stomach had contained no food at all, he had instead found a hard, gritty material, which proved to be cat litter.

The doctor also clarified that a subdural haematoma, due to blunt force trauma, could not have been caused accidentally, such as by falling, and that Gabriel hadn't received any medical treatment for his injuries.

Dr Ribe had concluded that the manner of death was homicide.

§

Despite the horrific torture he endured at the hands of his mother and her boyfriend in the last eight months of his life, Gabriel was loved by many.

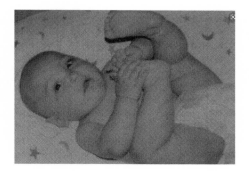

Beautiful baby

In every picture I have seen of Gabriel as a baby or toddler, he is brimming with joy and the confidence that comes from being loved. Raised from just three days old (summoned by Pearl Fernandez with the words: "Come and get your kid, he's getting on my nerves already") by his great-uncle Michael Lemos Carranza and his partner David Martinez, the love they shared is there for all to see.

But someone reported that Gabriel had been molested by his uncle.

With his Uncle Mike

These unsubstantiated claims appear to have offset the chain of events that led to Gabriel being taken from his uncles' loving care at the age of four, and into his grandparents' home. By all accounts, Robert and Sandra Fernandez also provided a stable and welcoming environment, with Gabriel playing in their swimming pool and riding his bike, along with his siblings and cousins. Again, photographs from that time show a happy and contented little boy.

Gabriel's father, Arnold Contreras, was in prison at the time of his son's murder. Blaming himself, he apologises to Gabriel on the witness stand during Aguirre's trial, believing that if he had not been in custody at the time, he could've saved his son.

George Carranza, the brother of Sandra and Michael, is featured in the Netflix docu-series on the case, The Trials of Gabriel Fernandez, along with his wife Elizabeth. Remembering Gabriel as playful, smiling, and always wanting to help, showing empathy beyond his years.

Elizabeth Carranza also recalls that Michael and David were good parents: "They would take him everywhere, and he would always be clean and happy … as a baby, he was always smiling. They loved being with him and raising him, and Gabriel loved them both very much."

When Pearl's new boyfriend appeared on the scene, Elizabeth thought he was a good hard-working man. He had a car, wasn't involved in gangs or drugs, and she hoped he might be good for her niece.

When they became concerned about Pearl's treatment of her son, the Carranzas called social workers at least three times and the sheriffs twice. Regarding the incident of the sheriff's deputy who visited the home after one such call-out and warned Gabriel about telling lies (more of this later), in the words of the Carranzas: "Why did they all believe Pearl over the kid with the marks?"

Numerous other family members loved Gabriel and spent happy times with him, and would've saved him from Pearl and Isauro if they could.

In the aftermath of horrific cases such as this, relatives of murdered children are sometimes vilified. But if the perpetrators keep them at a distance, or reports they make to the authorities are not adequately followed up, blaming those who are already grieving can be cruel and unjustified.

Apart from loving family, there are two people who, for me, stand out as compassionate voices for Gabriel. The first is Jennifer Garcia, his teacher at Summerwind Elementary School. She described Gabriel as a nice little boy, doing well in school, scoring A's for his work, and receiving an award for reading.

But Garcia was shocked one day, when Gabriel asked her: "Is it normal for your mom to hit you with a belt? And is it normal to bleed?" and she promptly called the child abuse hotline.

The young social worker assigned to the case rang her back. But it doesn't appear that the next step – the injuries to be seen by a medical practitioner – was carried out.

Before long, Gabriel started being absent from school, and he told a classmate that Aguirre was hitting him. His behaviour progressed from polite and kind to being bad tempered.

Ms Garcia noticed that chunks of Gabriel's hair were cut out, and he had bloody cuts on his head and ear and a fat lip. Gabriel told her that his mom had punched him. When Garcia approached the school principal to try and get further help for Gabriel, she was told: "We don't investigate, we just report".

Garcia reported to DCFS several times, but she noticed that Gabriel was becoming more withdrawn, and didn't want to go out and play, but instead stayed indoors and helped the teachers. He also said: "I don't want to go home. Can you call that lady?" And he cried and said he didn't want to get on the bus.

On one occasion, Garcia questioned Gabriel about his swollen eyes and bruised face. At first, the little boy said he fell when playing. When asked again, he got angry and said: "My mom shot me in the face with a BB gun, okay?" Tragically, he also said: "When I tell you and that lady comes, I get hurt worse". This made Jennifer Garcia hesitate, but she did report again.

After Gabriel returned to school after an absence of 13 days, one of his eyes was completely bloodshot red, and there was skin peeling off his forehead. He told his teacher that he had fallen off his bike. She called the social worker again but her call wasn't returned.

For a school Mother's Day Project, two weeks before his death, along with the other children, Gabriel made a card with a drawing of a house, and the poignant words: open the door to see who loves you. His photo was inside. He also wrote: She's a loving mom, and I love her because she's beautiful. Mother's Day Coupons had the words: I will be good. I will clean the dishes. A time for me and you.

Like so many abused children, even to the very end, Gabriel hoped that Fernandez would return his love.

At sentencing, Jennifer Garcia gave a simple but poignant victim impact statement, saying that she had not assigned Gabriel's pupil number – 28 – to any other student, as a way of honouring and remembering her young pupil.

§

The second person I want to mention, who was alarmed at the sight of Gabriel and tried to get help for him, was Arturo Miranda Martinez, who worked as a security guard at a local welfare office. When Pearl Fernandez arrived with her children, Martinez knew something was wrong with the smallest boy. He particularly noticed cigarette burns on the back of his head, and as he walked by, Gabriel made a fist in a desperate attempt to show that he was being punched.

Martinez alerted a colleague, who in turn made an attempt to report to her supervisor. Unfortunately, the supervisor could not, or would not, pay the overtime it would need to investigate, as the office was near to closing time. Arturo then rang 911 but was roughly told that a child with burns wasn't an emergency and to call the sheriff's office. It is believed that two deputies then visited the home, but as we know, nothing of value was done.

§

There were numerous opportunities to save Gabriel, and as happens frequently in child abuse murder cases, social services departments are pilloried, sometimes with significant justification.

This case is well known for the unusual step of criminal charges being brought against four social workers: child endangerment resulting in death, and falsification of documents. Many observers blame them for Gabriel's death, and they certainly acted in ways that left Gabriel vulnerable to his mother's cruelty.

The family were first under observation by the Department of Child and Family Services (DCFS) when Pearl's oldest child was born, after which there were numerous other reports made.

The following incident seems particularly remiss. When a volunteer with The Antelope Valley Children's Centre was visiting Pearl and Gabriel, Pearl handed her a note as she was on the verge of leaving. The note, written by Gabriel to his mother, read: "I love you so much that I will kill myself". Another read: "I love you until you die".

Alarmed at the eight-year-old's words, the volunteer called the child welfare hotline. But the recipient of the call spoke only to Pearl, not Gabriel. The hotline staff member's priority was whether Gabriel currently wanted to commit suicide, and she and his mother decided between them that there was no imminent risk. And tragically, this was not adequately followed up by either child protection or the police.

Those involved with the family said that they felt stressed and overworked, but added: "Why didn't we see it?"

Undoubtedly, one of the four social workers was assigned above her level of experience to the Fernandez case, and her supervisor did not check sufficiently that she had carried out the required procedures.

Furthermore, she was involved with the family from only 30 October 2012 to 31 January 2013, following which several other social workers and police officers saw the family, but they did not remove Gabriel nor arrest his mother or her boyfriend.

One such social worker discussed with Pearl about Gabriel acting up at school, but failed to investigate why he was doing so. She closed the case in April, but recorded that she had closed it in March, presumably so that she wouldn't appear to be responsible for anything that happened in that final month.

Eventually, the charges against the four social workers were dismissed, as it was said they were not required to control the abusers, nor did they have to care for the child themselves.

But Elizabeth Bartholet, Director of The Child Advocacy Program at Harvard Law School, has these damning words for Child and Family Services: "Very little emphasis on child rights" and "The system is broken because it is based on the wrong premise – **valuing adult rights way more than the child's**".

This happens time and again in child murder by maltreatment. A child's rights are seen as inferior to those of an adult, and to me, this fundamental imbalance is one of the primary reasons that so many children suffer and die at the hands of their 'caregivers'.

§

Unlike social work departments, the police, who also have a major role to play in protecting children, often fly under the radar.

After being forced to hand over a damning Internal Affairs report into the actions of the deputies of the Palmdale Sheriff's Station, all the deputies who visited Gabriel's home were subpoenaed.

It is not surprising that the information was handed over with such reluctance.

Sheriff's deputies had visited the home eight times in eight months, repeatedly swallowing Pearl Fernandez' explanations, and not asking to see Gabriel. Those who visited claimed to find no evidence of abuse, and crucially, reports that would have led to further investigations were not filed.

Although nine deputies were disciplined internally, none were fired or prosecuted, including the deputy who visited the home after Ms Garcia had reported that Gabriel had not attended school for several days. He believed Fernandez' explanation that her son had gone to live in Texas. No report was filed, and a week later, Gabriel was dead.

Another deputy had described Gabriel as a "spoiled kid who didn't get his way" after he spoke to Fernandez and Aguirre at 2am one morning. The officer then returned at

7am "to scare him" against making claims against his mother and her boyfriend. Putting him in the back of his car, he told Gabriel that if he kept lying about things he'd be sent to jail. Yes, you read that correctly; this individual threatened the bruised and battered eight-year-old, whose family was well-known to social workers and the police, with jail-time.

The "mis-steps" by law enforcement were viewed as "minor". The department declined to be interviewed for the Netflix documentary, *The Trials of Gabriel Fernandez*.

§

Why did Fernandez and Aguirre torture and ultimately beat Gabriel to death? Was Pearl an evil sociopath, a drug addict and temptress who held power over her boyfriend? Was Isauro jealous of Pearl giving attention to Gabriel instead of him?

In common with the majority of abusers, Pearl Fernandez seems to have had a turbulent childhood, perhaps involving abuse. Family members say that her father spent time in jail, and that she felt her mother did not love her.

It is said that Pearl began abusing methamphetamine and alcohol at just nine years old, ran away from home when she was eleven, dropped out of school at around the age of thirteen, and she claims that she was held hostage for several days, with a number of men taking turns to rape her. If true, these events would certainly pave the way for a disturbed young woman.

By contrast, what little we know of Isauro Aguirre portrays him in a different light. It is reported that he came from a poorly educated but hardworking family. Aguirre himself had repeated two grades of school and later dropped out, and it's possible that, as was alleged about Fernandez by her defence team, he was also intellectually challenged. His sister Elizabeth said that he "had been a caring and helpful older brother", who had been an altar boy when he was younger and had gone to church regularly. (Of course, this is not proof of empathy and kindness.)

Two former girlfriends testified that he was "helpful and respectful," although following one break-up, he made a nuisance of himself by repeatedly calling his ex. His defence team argued that Aguirre had no prior criminal history and suggested that he was corrupted by Pearl Fernandez.

Aguirre had worked for over three years as a driver and caregiver at Woodland Park retirement home, with his former boss describing him as kind and caring, and popular with the residents, who often requested that he care for them.

But Aguirre's lack of emotion or remorse during the trial helped to convince the jury that he was guilty of murder in the 1st degree. With the special circumstance of torture, they voted in favour of the death penalty, and he currently resides on Death Row in St Quentin prison.

At her pre-trial hearing, Fernandez pleaded guilty to the same charges, thereby avoiding trial by jury. She was sentenced to life in prison without the possibility of parole. She is incarcerated in Chowchilla State Women's Prison.

At the hearing, Fernandez read out a few words, apologising to her kids. She said that she wished Gabriel was alive, and that she'd *made better choices*. She also said she hoped her kids would "*come to their senses*" and go visit her.

Gabriel is one of the 6-7 million children in the US who are victims of alleged abuse or neglect every year, and one of around 1,800 children whose torture ends in murder.

That's five children, in the US alone, suffering and dying like Gabriel, every day.

Gabriel's legacy lives on in the hearts of those who want to end child abuse and murder.

Gabriel's House, a community arts facility offering music, visual and performing arts to children in the area in which Gabriel lived with his murderers, was set up in his memory. At the time of writing, I believe it is temporarily closed, but there are plans to re-open, in partnership with the 'Music and Kids' enterprise.

Along with murals in his honour, Gabriel's Tree, close to his Palmdale home, is a gathering place for many who remember the kind, gentle, and loving little boy. There is a wonderful Facebook group called Gabriel's Tree, A Tribute to Gabriel Fernandez and Child Abuse Victims, of which I am proud to be a member.

And family members founded the Facebook group, Gabriel's Justice, which along with two other excellent groups, Letters for Gabriel Fernandez, and Justice for Gabriel Fernandez, offers a space where those who care about Gabriel can find like-minded people who want to raise awareness of Gabriel's story, and of other children who are Abused To Death.

Tragically, Gabriel's great-uncle Mike died of cancer 16 months after Gabriel died, and Mike's partner, David, died as a result of contracting Covid-19 in July 2020. Those who believe in a heavenly afterlife take comfort in the belief that the family are together again, along with Sandra, his grandmother, who died from complications of diabetes.

His name is Gabriel Fernandez.

Please don't forget him.

How can we protect children like Gabriel?

Thank You For Reading

When I first started my research, I couldn't believe what I was reading, and I shed many tears for the children. Only getting my feelings down on paper helped me to get to sleep at night, and so I began to write the children's stories.

I still find each case really upsetting, as I'm sure you do, and I feel that much more should be done to protect the children. It's not easy, but there *are* things we can all do.

> If you feel you'd also like to raise awareness, a rating or review for this book can really make an immense difference.

And I'd love to hear from you, so if you have any comments or suggestions, please get in touch: **jessicajackson@jesstruecrime.com**

MY NAME IS GABRIEL FERNANDEZ

Help To Protect Children Like Gabriel

Please just review in your usual way, or the QR code or link should help you to get back to the book's page:

mybook.to/GabrielFernandez

Then scroll **waaay down**
until you see **Write a Review**
(usually on the left side)

Reviews help to spread the word about abuse and I appreciate every single one. Just a star rating or a few words is enough.

Your Next Book in the Series

Are you ready for more stories like Gabriel's?

Volume 1 of my main series covers eight cases, including Sylvia Likens, and Baby P.

Find your copy in your usual way or:

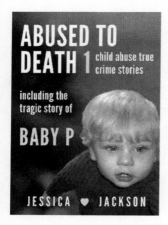

Just scan this code:

Or use this link:

mybook.to/Abused-To-Death-1

Join Us On Facebook

Want to connect with me and join a community of people who want to prevent child abuse?

I honour the murdered children on my Facebook page, and if you'd like to come and say 'Hi' on one of my posts, it'd be great to see you there.

If you wish, you can **Follow, Like & Share** my posts.

Just scan this code:

Or use this link:

https://www.facebook.com/AbusedToDeath/

Or within Facebook, type into the search bar:

Jessica Jackson – Writer Against Abuse

An Invitation

Would you like to **join my Readers' List**, by picking up your free ebook overleaf?

And would you please do me a great favour?

*Because my books are so sad, I double-check that you want to join my Readers' List, and so you'll receive a quick email from me, to ask you to **confirm your place**.*

> *Can you please reply either **Yes or No** to this email? It only takes a few seconds but is **incredibly** helpful to me.*

If you don't receive the email almost instantly, please check Junk/Spam – I can't add you without your reply.

Thank you; I really appreciate this.

Readers' List Benefits

Members get special offers, along with each new release at the subscriber price. And if you'd like to be more involved, you can **suggest children to include**, give your input on cover design, and lots more.

I'm always interested in what my readers think, and so on the day after you've confirmed your place and joined us, I'll email you with the question:

"ARE THEY MONSTERS?"

I'd love to include your opinion in my readers' poll.

Then I'll leave you in peace for a while!

So, get your free ebook overleaf, and thank you in advance if you decide to join us.

Pick Up Your Free Ebook and Join Us!

Isaiah Torres was just six years old when he was abused to death in the most appalling way.

Pick up your copy of your free ebook

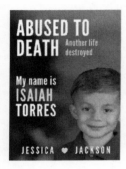

Just scan this code:

Or use this link:

https://BookHip.com/VNGMZJJ

Then be sure to click Yes or No on the quick email I'll send to confirm your place – it looks like this:

Yes thanks, I'd love to join, Jess

OR

No, I won't join just now, Jess

Find All My Books on Amazon

Find them in your usual way, or you can ...

Search Amazon for:

Abused To Death by Jessica Jackson

Or scan this code:

Or use this link:

viewbook.at/abused-series

If you wish, you can also **Follow** me on Amazon.

MY NAME IS GABRIEL FERNANDEZ

My Latest Book

Abused To Death Volume 4

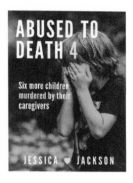

Just scan this code:

- Adrian Jones endured unspeakable torture, and after his death, his body was fed to pigs

- Hana Williams was adopted from Ethiopia by those who believed they were doing God's work

- Maxwell Schollenberger was hidden away, year after year, in a filthy attic

Don't miss a thing:

Follow me on Facebook:
https://www.facebook.com/AbusedToDeath/

Pick up your free book about Isaiah Torres and join my Readers' List:
https://BookHip.com/VNGMZJJ

Follow me on Amazon:
viewbook.at/abused-series

Prevention

Abuse and murder occur for complex reasons, and prevention is an immense task. These are my own views on how we can move towards prevention of this horrendous crime, echoing those of the World Health Organisation (WHO).

1 - End physical discipline of children
2 - Regulate homeschooling effectively
3 - An outlet for caregivers' anger
4 - Listen to the children when they report abuse
5 - Improve communication between agencies
6 - Safe places for unwanted babies
7 - Educate the parents of the future:
- that a baby communicates by crying
- how to give love, safety and guidance
- about bladder & bowel habits of children

Warning Signs of Abuse

There are various factors that might suggest a child is being abused. This list has been compiled by the NSPCC, but is not exhaustive:
- unexplained changes in behaviour or personality
- becoming withdrawn or anxious
- becoming uncharacteristically aggressive
- lacking social skills and having few friends
- poor bonding or relationship with a parent
- knowledge of issues inappropriate for their age
- running away or going missing
- wearing clothes which cover their body

And I would add:

- marks and bruises on the body
- being secretive
- stealing (often food)
- weight loss
- inappropriate clothing
- poor hygiene / unkempt
- tiredness
- inability to concentrate
- being overly eager to please the adult
- the child *telling* you that they're being hurt
  (alarmingly, this is often ignored)
- a non-verbal child *showing* you that they're being hurt

- the adult removing the child from school after they have come under suspicion

And when faced with an adult who you suspect of abusing a child, don't unquestioningly accept what they say, but instead:

> **A** - Assume nothing
>
> **B** - Be vigilant
>
> **C** - Check everything
>
> **D** - Do something

Listen to the children and report what you see

TO REPORT CHILD ABUSE IN THE USA & CANADA

The National Child Abuse Hotline:1-800-422-4453

If a child is in immediate danger, call 911

TO REPORT CHILD ABUSE IN THE UK

Adults, call the NSPCC on 0808 800 5000

Children, call Childline on 0800 1111

Or if there is risk of imminent danger, ring 999

TO REPORT CHILD ABUSE IN AUSTRALIA

The National Child Abuse Reportline: 131-478
Children, call: 1800-55-1800
If a child is in immediate danger, call 000

Selected Resources

- Netflix Series 'The Trials of Gabriel Fernandez'
- Court reports
- Numerous newspaper articles, notably those by Garrett Therolf, LA Times

Acknowledgments

WITH GRATEFUL THANKS TO:

- My beta readers: Jackson, Linda and Rick
- All my email subscribers, old and new
- My Facebook followers
- My incredible Advance Readers
- My fellow authors Ryan Green and Jason Neal
- And for much needed light relief, my friend and comedy crime writer, Roy M Burgess

Disclaimer

My aim is to tell stories of murdered children with a combination of accuracy and readability, to heighten awareness of child torture and murder, and to explore ways of preventing further tragedies. I have relied on the factual information available to me during my research, and where I have added characters or dramatised events to better tell the child's story, I believe I have done so without significantly altering the important details. If anyone has further information about the children, particularly if you knew them and have anecdotes to share about their life, I would be delighted to hear from you. Likewise, whilst every attempt has been made to make contact with copyright holders, if I have unwittingly used any material when I was not at liberty to do so, please contact me so that this can be rectified at:

jessicajackson@jesstruecrime.com

Made in the USA
Columbia, SC
25 September 2024

43027929R00055